HOPPER'S PLACES

GAIL LEVIN

HOPPER'S PLACES

Alfred A. Knopf   New York   1985

In honor of my mother, who taught me to love painting,

and in memory of my father, who taught me to love books

THIS IS A BORZOI BOOK
PUBLISHED BY ALFRED A. KNOPF, INC.

Library of Congress Cataloging in Publication Data
Levin, Gail, 1948–
Hopper's places.
1. Hopper, Edward, 1882–1967. 2. United States in art.
I. Title.
ND237.H75L484   1985   759.13   85-40039
ISBN 0-394-54414-5
ISBN 0-394-72228-0 (pbk.)

Manufactured in The Netherlands
First Edition

CONTENTS

HOPPER'S PLACES

I began photographing places Hopper painted quite by chance. During the late 1960s, I spent a Thanksgiving vacation with a college classmate in Portland, Maine. Showing me around her hometown, she drove me out to Cape Elizabeth to see the lighthouse at Two Lights, which had been painted, she proudly informed me, by the artist Edward Hopper. I had been greatly impressed by Hopper's work, examples of which I had seen in the Museum of Fine Arts in Boston, and decided at once to take a picture of his motif. I also photographed my friend standing before the lighthouse. At the time I was both an art and an art history major and had been painting my own Cape Cod landscapes in a realist style inspired by Hopper.

I routinely tucked these snapshots away in an album, never dreaming that I would later spend eight years as curator of this artist's estate at the Whitney Museum of American Art, where I organized major Hopper exhibitions and wrote a catalogue raisonné, a definitive study of the artist's work, as well as articles, books, and catalogue essays. I approached my work there with great enthusiasm and thoroughness. So much so, that a male journalist who interviewed me in 1980 in Milwaukee, on the occasion of the opening of a Hopper exhibition that I had curated, incorrectly concluded: "The man in Gail Levin's life has been dead for thirteen years" (Hopper had died in 1967, just before his eighty-fifth birthday). Perhaps this journalist would

have been even more perplexed had he known of my travels tracing Hopper's footsteps, searching out the very sights he had painted.

This idea began not only in my chance encounter with the lighthouse on Cape Elizabeth but also in an experience I had had during the previous year while I was studying in Paris. On spring vacation, I had taken an overnight train south to Aix-en-Provence to meet a friend. This was my first visit to the south of France, and although I was quite familiar with the great painting that had been produced there, I did not expect the actual landscape to resemble so closely these icons of modern art. Rather I imagined that artists such as van Gogh and Cézanne had created their images more from their imaginations and sources in other art such as Japanese prints. Awakened in the early morning just at sunrise, I stood looking out the train window in amazement at the landscape of Provence with its cypresses and orchards with gnarled tree-trunks so evocative of van Gogh. My stay in Aix, where I visited Cézanne's studio and saw some of the places that he had painted, reinforced this impression. How these artists had responded to the world around them and captured it in their canvases!

I soon discovered the 1943 book *Cézanne's Composition*, by the painter Erle Loran, as well as his original article "Cézanne's Country," published in the April 1930 issue of *The Arts*, where the first photographs of the artist's motifs appeared. Later I delved into the pioneering work on Cézanne by the art historian John Rewald, who published his photographs of Cézanne's sites in a number of articles, including a marvelous essay, "The Last Motifs at Aix," which appeared in the catalogue of the 1977 exhibition at the Museum of Modern Art, *Cézanne: The Late Work*. This last article reinforced the value of such precise documentation in the context of my own research on Hopper.

Rewald described how he and his friend, the painter Leo Marchutz, had, against the property owner's wishes, surreptitiously cut off tree branches in order to "'liberate' views of the buildings which they obstructed." He also lamented how rapidly things changed, eradicating Cézanne's views forever: "Forest fires ruined some sites, new construction others." This, in fact, predicted my own experience with Hopper's places. Sometimes, the extensive growth of landscaping trees and bushes conceals the structures Hopper painted, rendering them all but unrecognizable; elsewhere, the sprawling growth of suburbia has crept up on the most tranquil of locales. I have witnessed these dramatic changes even in the relatively short time I have been visiting and documenting Hopper's places, particularly at the lighthouse at Two Lights on Cape Elizabeth (which I have visited intermittently now for over sixteen years), where new construction now blocks some of the vistas that once delighted him.

Perhaps in America, where Hopper painted, change is even more rapid and drastic than that observed by Rewald in the south of France. Here we tend to praise such uncontrolled growth and call it progress. In this sense, both painters and photographers of cityscapes and landscapes serve the function of creating a permanent record of the appearance of places that are subject to constant transformation.

And to understand a realist painter like Hopper, we must explore both his choice of subject matter and his method of depiction. Just how faithful to his observations was he? One accurate way to assess this aspect of his work is to compare his actual subjects, where they survive, to their appearances in the paintings themselves. Born in 1882, Hopper began in his boyhood to sketch and paint motifs in his environment; by the 1910s, he had returned from his travels abroad and had seriously begun to record the world around him. Thus, it was none too soon that I began to photograph Hopper's sites, some of which no longer existed and some of which have changed beyond recognition since I photographed them. In most cases, by the time I arrived at these places, camera in hand, decades had passed since Hopper had painted there; but fortunately he was attracted to backwater locations where the force of progress has been gentler than might be expected.

In this volume, I have decided to focus on Hopper's most important American places—New York City and its environs; Maine; Gloucester, Massachusetts; and Cape Cod—for it is in these locations, in the places he knew best, that his work is most revealing. I have treated his response to Paris and Mexico in articles in *Arts Magazine* (June 1979) and *Geo* (February 1983). Other places to which he traveled—Santa Fe, New Mexico; Charleston, South Carolina; and parts of Wyoming, Oregon, and California—could also have been included. Rather than end up with a travelogue, however, I have chosen to investigate the most significant locales more thoroughly, attempting to illuminate the artist's motivations and working procedure.

HOPPER'S SUBJECTS

Edward Hopper (1882–1967), the quintessential realist painter of twentieth-century America, portrayed the commonplace and made the ordinary poetic. In choosing his subjects, from rural New England (Maine, Vermont, Cape Ann, and Cape Cod) to South Carolina, New Mexico, and New York City and its environs, Hopper was drawn to stark architectural vistas which he usually emptied of human figures—spare compositions and situations evoking feelings of loneliness and solitude.

Hopper's realism was not merely a literal or photographic copying of what he saw but an interpretive rendering of the settings he depicted. His choice of subjects is well worth examining, for therein lies an important clue to the very nature of Hopper's vision. The places that Hopper painted reveal much about his personality, his tastes, and the cultural climate of his time.

One of the most frequently recurring images in Hopper's oeuvre is a view of a body of water: seascapes and nautical scenes, lighthouses, harbors, rivers, bridges, and even the view from his summer home in Truro, Massachusetts, overlooking Cape Cod Bay. Having grown up quite near the Hudson River in Nyack, New York, Hopper was always drawn to water, which may have symbolized freedom and escape for this reclusive artist. As an adolescent, he had been encouraged by his father to build a sailboat, evidently so that he would get outside and be less of an introvert. Later Hopper admitted that he had considered a career as a naval architect; sailing remained a lifelong passion. The many lighthouses he painted may reflect a certain identification on his part: he was nearly six feet five inches tall and perhaps felt a special affinity to this genre of architecture, which, like him, stood apart, detached from the rest of the world.

While Hopper's architectural subjects are generally devoid of human figures, it was not until 1940 that his imagery was specifically described as "lonely." This subsequently prompted critics to make retrospective assessments of the art he had produced in the previous two decades. Hopper himself, asked to explain the absence of figures in *Macomb's Dam Bridge* (1935), a painting that depicts New York, a city of millions of people, offered: "I don't know why except that they say I am lonely."

Hopper's empty places and solitary figures repeatedly suggested pangs of loneliness to a public increasingly interested in psychoanalytic thought and aware of the growing anonymity of contemporary urban life. By 1964, these interpretations of his work forced Hopper to insist that "the loneliness thing is overdone," although that same year he responded to an interviewer's assessment of "profound loneliness" and a lack of communication in his art with the comment: "It's probably a reflection of my own, if I may say, loneliness. I don't know. It could be the whole human condition." As early as 1923, Hopper titled an etching *The Lonely House*; but since the composition includes two children, the title suggests a larger, more existential loneliness —a kind of societal isolation. This is similar to the sense of estrangement present in his oil painting *House by the Railroad* (1925, Fig. 6) or in his various paintings of isolated lighthouses.

Perhaps Hopper's alienation results from his reclusive personality, which, as noted earlier, was already established in childhood. He felt a frustration in human relationships that he communicated in his art, not only through melancholy solitary figures but also through metaphors for escape (trains, highways) and through the depiction of so many empty places, often where we would expect people to be present. In this sense, we must recognize that a painting like *Solitude* (1944) reflects Hopper's preference for empty spaces over the company of others, which he found difficult to accept.

Hopper's associations with the particular architecture he chose to paint are more complex. The early twentieth century was an era of burgeoning nationalism, and typical American scenes do appear as the subjects of his art. His hometown, Nyack, offered examples of architectural styles characteristic of nineteenth-century America. Although these styles were passively absorbed by Hopper in his youth, it was not until after he traveled abroad, between 1906 and 1910, that he fully came to appreciate their charm. Writing in *The Arts* in 1927, Hopper commented on contemporary American artists whose work he admired and stressed the necessity of developing a "native art," reiterating a point many critics were then noting about his own work: "The 'tang of the soil' is becoming evident more and more in their painting....We should not be quite certain of the crystallization of the art of America into something native and distinct, were it not that our drama, our literature and our architecture show very evident signs of doing just that thing."

For example, Hopper was especially fond of the kind

of roof so frequently found on American houses of the Second Empire style, built between 1860 and 1890. This style, which like its name is borrowed from French architecture developed during the reign of Napoleon III, is characterized by a mansard roof covered with multicolored slates or tinplates. In 1907 and 1909, Hopper had made several paintings of the Pavillon de Flore of the Louvre, which he could see from the corner where he lived on Paris's Left Bank. He undoubtedly admired the mansard roof of this elegant building and later must have been attracted to similar roof structures on American houses, which he depicted in watercolors such as *The Mansard Roof* (1923, Pl. 11), *Haskell's House* (1924, Fig. 2), and *Talbot's House* (1926, Pl. 4), as well as in his oils *House by the Railroad* (Fig. 6) and *The Bootleggers,* both of 1925. Since Hopper found these houses in a variety of locations—Gloucester, Massachusetts; Rockland, Maine; and probably New York state—it appears that he actually sought each of them out because of his fascination with the intricate mansard roof, flanked by classical moldings and ornamental details such as cornices and arched windows.

Although it seems at first glance that Hopper was routinely drawn to the most ordinary of buildings, there is inevitably something special about the subjects he selected—often a personal preference or specific

Fig. 1. *Haunted House*, 1926, watercolor on paper, 14 × 20″.

8 association. For instance, in 1926, visiting Rockland, Maine, he had stumbled upon a deserted boarding-house at 5 South Street, near the town's shipyard. Old photographs document Hopper's verisimilitude to this subject, now long since destroyed. Despite its ordinary structure, Hopper was drawn to its state of abandonment, noting particularly its boarded-up windows and even titling his watercolor *Haunted House* (Fig. 1)—although the work has subsequently been known as *Old Boarding House,* masking the substance of the artist's original preoccupation with what must reflect his growing fascination with death. This morbidity and his characteristic pessimism are also indicated by Hopper's predilection for painting watercolors of houses surrounded by dead trees: *Dead Trees* (1923), *Dead Tree and Side of Lombard House* (1931), *House with Dead Tree* (1932) and *Four Dead Trees* (1942).

Hopper occasionally selected architectural subjects of greater aesthetic distinction. This was particularly true in 1927, during his stay in Portland, Maine, where he chose to paint watercolors of a distinguished high Victorian mansion and the elegant granite United States Custom House built in 1872 in a Grecian style. These choices were in sharp contrast to some of the more commonplace buildings that he had painted, just one year earlier, in Rockland, Maine.

His choices of subject matter—particularly the places he painted—seem to have been somewhat un-predictable, since they were part of his constant battle with the chronic boredom that often stifled his urge to paint. This is what kept Hopper on the move—his search for inspiration, least painfully found in the stimulation of new surroundings. As he explained to one critic: "To me the most important thing is the sense of going on. You know how beautiful things are when you're traveling."

HOPPER'S METHOD

As a young man just out of art school, Hopper first traveled to Paris in the fall of 1906 and remained there until the following summer. He then visited London and ventured across Europe, stopping off in Haarlem, Amsterdam, Berlin, and Brussels. After a second trip to Paris in the spring and summer of 1909, he toured Spain during June 1910 before passing the last weeks he would ever spend in Paris. Back home in America, as a struggling young artist reluctantly working as an illustrator, Hopper (according to what little is known of his life at this time) still managed to spend most of his summers in the country, away from the steaming streets of New York. He went to Gloucester, Massachusetts, in 1912; to Ogunquit, Maine, in 1914 and 1915; and to Monhegan Island, twelve miles off the coast of Maine, every summer from 1916 to 1919.

It was a return to Gloucester during the summer of 1923 that changed Hopper's direction. There he ran into Josephine Nivison, who, like him, had studied with Robert Henri at the New York School of Art. Nivison had already exhibited her watercolors in New York, and she encouraged Hopper, who had used the medium only as a boy and, more recently, for his commercial work, to try working in watercolor that summer on painting excursions they made together. She also recognized his unusual facility and respected his ability. When she received an invitation to show her watercolors in a group show at the Brooklyn Museum that fall, she told the museum about Hopper's new work in the medium, prompting his inclusion in the exhibition. This exhibition resulted in the museum's purchase of *The Mansard Roof,* Hopper's first sale of a painting in a decade, and brought him much favorable publicity. Perhaps Hopper, then aged forty-one, realized that he had at last found his best ally; he married Jo the next summer, and they spent their honeymoon back in Gloucester, painting watercolors.

Hopper painted his watercolors directly while looking at his subjects, which were almost always outdoor scenes: ships, the seashore, a lighthouse, a church, streets, houses, and trees. Having worked in watercolor as an illustrator, he handled the medium with confidence. After outlining his composition with a pale pencil sketch, he improvised as the work progressed, focusing on the recording of sunlight, interested in structure rather than texture. The result of Hopper's improvisatory technique is a spontaneity that does not occur in his oil paintings, a contrast that is especially notable when one compares the occasional oils that Hopper painted based on earlier watercolor compositions.

Before 1927, when Jo and Edward purchased their first automobile, Hopper's daily watercolor expeditions were usually on foot, and he was subject to wind and rain and other inconveniences. Their first car—they always bought them second-hand—provided not only transportation but also a mobile studio. With the front seat pushed forward to accommodate his long legs, Edward worked in the backseat behind the steering wheel, while petite Jo, nestled next to the driver's seat, produced her own watercolors or sketches. Despite his thrifty nature, Hopper always insisted on replacing any windshield of tinted glass so that he could see his surroundings in their proper tonality.

In Paris, Hopper had painted all his oils outdoors on location. Of course, during the cold rainy months of winter, this limited his production. He found other diversions for this time, however, and he frequently sketched in cafés, endlessly observing the French who provoked his fantasies. Back in America, Hopper had already begun to improvise, painting on occasion in the studio from memory or his imagination. He continued to work outdoors during the summers that he spent in rural New England, evidently often sketching and painting directly on the canvas without making separate preliminary sketches.

Increasingly, though, Hopper began to make pencil or charcoal drawings on location, sometimes recording notes about color observations. These drawings were always done in monochrome, usually black and white but occasionally red Conté crayon. By the late 1930s, all of his canvases were produced in the studio; many were syntheses of several places Hopper had observed and sketched. For example, *New York Movie* (1939) combines drawings made at several theaters with sketches of Jo posing as the usherette in the hallway of their apartment building. Hopper never gave up working from observation; but as old age and infirmity made traveling about more difficult, he adapted by transforming his surroundings through the filter of his imagination.

HOPPER'S COMPOSITION

Photographs of the sites Hopper painted demonstrate how closely he followed nature. Nonetheless, they also reveal how on occasion he freely altered what he observed. He could subtly change the spatial organization of a composition from that which he could objec-

tively see to one that better suited his purpose. It is important to consider when and just how much Hopper chose to manipulate nature, how he selected his eye level or horizon line and his point of view, what decisions he made about the cropping of images, and how much he distorted scale and shape to suit his expressive needs.

Although Hopper did not work from photographs (except occasionally in his early commercial illustrations), he did admit to having once purchased a camera in order to take pictures of architectural details. The results of the camera disappointed him because, he recalled, "the camera sees things from a different angle, not like the eye." He explained to fellow painter Raphael Soyer that images in photographs "do not have enough weight." Hopper did, however, admire "how much personality a good photographer can get into a picture," and he specifically singled out the work of the French photographer Eugène Atget, whose work he probably first discovered in Paris. Atget's solitary, empty spaces and melancholy mood must have appealed to Hopper as they echoed his own vision.

In *Davis House* (1926, Pl. 14), Hopper compresses the foreground in size, omitting the intervention of the street that lies between the house and the fence bordering the churchyard where he was working. By cropping the house abruptly on the left side rather than including the entire structure, he suggests that the scene continues beyond the confines of his composition, adding an extra degree of realism to his verisimilitude.

By cropping the house in *Rooms for Tourists* (1945, Pl. 23) at the top of the composition, Hopper ensures that the viewer's eye does not wander up the triangular gable and out of the painting. Instead, he forces our attention back down into the center of the composition. He had also employed this device of cropping the top of an image in earlier works such as *Anderson's House* (Pl. 13), *Libby House* (Pl. 10), *Captain Strout's House* (Pl. 8), and *House on Middle Street* (Pl. 15).

More complicated was Hopper's use of multiple points of view, allowing the spectator to see his subject as it actually looked from several different positions. This seems to add to the sensation of realism, because it creates a sense of omniscience in the viewer, who can grasp more than could an actual spectator standing in a fixed location. For example, in *Rooms for Tourists,* which was constructed in the studio from drawings done on location, we see the side of the boardinghouse and the two houses on the adjoining right lot from the left, while the facade appears much more frontal. By appearing nearly parallel to the picture plane, the bordering hedge serves to emphasize this sense of frontality.

In *Davis House* Hopper's station point—his distance and position in relation to his subject—is also ambiguous. While the central house appears quite frontal, as if

he stood directly across from it, Hopper also utilized another vantage point, off to the left side, so that we look onto the side of the house next door. This is clarified when we examine the shadows in the watercolor. The gables on the roof of the central house cast shadows to the left of the composition, indicating that the sunlight is coming from the right side. At the same time, the concrete post on the fence is viewed from the left and inconsistently highlighted by a second light source coming from the left. The angle of vision is very low, perhaps because the artist was sitting on the ground, so that the viewer looks up under the eaves of the house.

Hopper often utilized an unusual angle of vision, either from an elevated position or from below his subject. The latter, often referred to as a worm's-eye view, includes works such as *The Mansard Roof, Haskell's House, Lighthouse at Two Lights, House on Dune Edge* (Fig. 3), or *Near the Back Shore* (Pl. 20). Here one senses the influence of Degas, whose work Hopper openly admired. Degas even wrote: "Equip the studio with benches arranged in tiers to inculcate the habit of drawing objects seen from above and from below." Although all of Hopper's positions were logically chosen according to the natural inclines of the surrounding landscape, he selected these vantage points intentionally, fully aware of Degas's proclivity for such compositions. The same is true of works painted from an elevated position or bird's-eye perspective: *Portland*

Head-Light (Pl. 7), *Dauphinée House* (Fig. 12), *November, Washington Square,* or *City Roofs* (Pl. 1).

Many of Hopper's subjects are viewed from an oblique angle off to the left side: *House by the Railroad; Anderson's House; House on Middle Street; Adam's House* (Pl. 17); *Prospect Street, Gloucester* (Pl. 16); *Rich's House* (Pl. 18)—to name only a few. Less frequently, he reversed this kind of composition and employed a view from the right-hand side: *Talbot's House, The Mansard Roof,* or *Haunted House.*

Hopper's inclusion of the rail-and-post fence in *Davis House* is not based on formal considerations alone. He used this fence as a psychological barrier, setting up a firm distancing device between himself and his subject. Characteristically, he did not allow himself (or the viewer) to become too involved or too threateningly intimate with the subjects in his paintings. This use of a fence as a barrier abounds in paintings such as *Haskell's House; Parkhurst House (Captain's House); Captain Strout's House* (Pl. 8); *Libby House; Custom House, Portland* (Pl. 9); *Rich's House;* and *Two Puritans.* In *Captain Strout's House,* although the original fence probably paralleled the house just as the present one does, Hopper placed it at an oblique angle in order to add a dynamic quality to the composition. Other barrier devices that he frequently used for both compositional and psychological purposes are railroad tracks and embankments, highways and roads, steep eleva-

tions in the landscape, and doorways and thresholds.

Hopper also took liberties in changing the relative proportions and even the shapes of his subjects. He most often made buildings appear to be more vertical than they are in reality. This tendency to elongate structures may have been the result of his subconscious identification with his own great height. Examples of this phenomenon can be seen in *Lighthouse Hill* (Pl. 5), *Captain Upton's House,* and *House on Middle Street,* where the actual houses are clearly broader than he chose to depict them. Sometimes Hopper flattened out forms as well. In *The Mansard Roof,* for example, we cannot really detect the angle where the two windows meet on the side of the house on the far right. Instead, Hopper, who in this early watercolor seems to have been preoccupied with the dramatic play of light and shadow, was willing to utilize compositional manipulations to achieve the look he wanted. In this he continued, developing subtle skills and effective devices.

FINDING HOPPER'S PLACES

My search for Hopper's places took many forms, from the most directed investigation to the serendipitous. I began by examining Hopper's paintings of easily identifiable places: *The Lighthouse at Two Lights;*

Macomb's Dam Bridge; Prospect Street, Gloucester; and *Custom House, Portland.* These places proved simple to locate and appeared relatively unchanged. In the process, I became familiar with Hopper's territory and began to understand what kind of places attracted him. I could say with confidence that Hopper might have painted this or would never have painted that.

As I collected photographs of all his known works for the catalogue raisonné, I discovered unpublished or little-known images which I then recognized while visiting the areas in which he painted. I found that he did tend to paint additional works while in the vicinity of another one of his subjects. I learned to think of Hopper's working method, whether he was on foot or in his automobile, and was able to find not only the locations he painted but the places where he worked. These discoveries in turn have led me to a greater understanding of how he selected the places he painted.

Familiarity with the record books kept by Jo, in which Hopper often made miniature sketches of his works, offered some further clues, although Hopper was usually vague about where in a given town a work was painted. In Gloucester, I had no trouble finding the subject of *House on Middle Street,* but the unidentified locations of so many other houses painted there presented greater challenges. Initially, just driving and walking around, I found a few of his sites. It helped to have a friend along to take the wheel, so that I could

Fig. 2. *Haskell's House,* 1924, watercolor on paper, 14 × 20″.

Fig. 3. *House on Dune Edge*, 1930, watercolor on paper, 14 × 20″.

keep my eyes on the houses. I recognized the model for *Anderson's House* while cruising by on the way to some other place. Stopping to take a photograph, I spoke to a man applying a coat of paint to the house's exterior: "Did you know that Edward Hopper once painted this house?" "All I know is that I'm painting it now," he replied—demolishing my fantasy that I had discovered a struggling artist working as a house painter on the very structure that Hopper had depicted.

Having found as much as I could on my own, I decided to visit a fire station because I figured the firemen would be likely to recognize existing buildings. When I showed photographs of Hopper's Gloucester paintings to a group of firemen, they looked at them with interest and offered various tentative suggestions until I came to *Adam's House*. One man perked up and offered: "I know that one—my mother lives in that house!" Of course I received a lot of false leads from well-meaning people at the firehouse and elsewhere: Hopper's paintings have a quintessential look about them and seem familiar even when they are not.

One of the problems was recognizing places that have been camouflaged since Hopper painted them. I had driven by the subject of *Haskell's House* (Fig. 2) many times before I recognized it. Although the house is distinctive, its shrubbery is missing, and large fir trees disguise the setting, now so radically changed by the transformation of Gloucester harbor. In North

Truro on Cape Cod, the model for *House on Dune Edge* has been so enlarged that the original distinctive round structure is now enclosed by the additions, totally changing the spirit of the place Hopper painted in 1931 (Fig. 3).

Another dilemma I faced was wasting time searching for places that might no longer exist. The abandoned Rockland boardinghouse of *Haunted House* (1926), the North Truro warehouse in *Cold Storage Plant* (1933, Fig. 5), and the South Truro train station in *Towards Boston* (1936, Fig. 4) had all been torn down, but there are old photographs that document Hopper's verisimilitude to these places. I found the photograph of the station on exhibit when I made a chance visit to the Museum of the Truro Historical Society.

Yet so many places Hopper painted have survived intact. I found old houses still standing in all the locales where he worked. In Paris, the building he lived in is unchanged, including the stairwell and inner courtyard, which he painted. In Saltillo, Mexico, I not only found the views Hopper recorded but visited the Hotel Arizpe Sainz, where he stayed. There I found that he had chosen a room with direct access to the roof, where he painted in an environment recalling his work on the top of 3 Washington Square North in New York. The El Palacio cinema, the architecture, and the mountains that he painted from his rooftop all remain.

I had much help in my search for Hopper's places

Fig. 4. *Towards Boston*, 1936, watercolor on paper, 14 × 20″.

from people who volunteered leads and made suggestions in response to my work on exhibitions and publications on the artist. The problem is that many people think they have found Hopper's places when in fact they have not. Countless individuals believe that they have seen the two-story buildings of *Early Sunday Morning* everywhere in Manhattan and Brooklyn, but Hopper's original title for this work—*Seventh Avenue Shops*—indicates that these have been cases of mistaken identity. The proprietor of a Greenwich Village candy store, about to be evicted when his landlord wanted to demolish his building, implored me to document that his shop was the location painted by Hopper in his 1942 masterpiece *Nighthawks* and should therefore be preserved. He was correct about his store being in the vicinity of the diner in *Nighthawks,* but the place Hopper described as having inspired him was surely on the empty triangular lot across the street.

Just north of Nyack, in the town of Haverstraw, New York, is a house resembling that in *House by the Railroad* (Fig. 6) of 1925. Situated just across the road from the train station, this massive example of the Second Empire style is complete with the mansard roof, central tower, front porch with double columns, and corniced windows that Hopper included in his painting.

Fig. 5. *Cold Storage Plant*, 1933, watercolor on paper, 24 × 12″.

While it is not known where the actual house Hopper painted was located, this one is certainly in a place that he could have seen. Although it is not as close to the train tracks, Hopper sometimes chose to compress space, making foreground distances disappear, as he did with the churchyard railing and street in his Gloucester watercolor *Davis House,* painted just a year later.

As Hopper had earlier invented the view out of the doorway in his family home in Nyack, we must ask if he did not also modify details in *House by the Railroad,* eliminating the surrounding buildings to create a sense of isolation. Did he extract only those essential parts of the structure that he needed and omit other, less significant architectural details to achieve greater simplicity and clarity? Although many different observers have suggested to me that the Haverstraw house was definitely the model for *House by the Railroad,* I must admit that I am not certain whether Hopper would have made such great changes in structural details as the double-story cornice on the now-projecting tower, at such an early date. If this is a case of mistaken identity, the house nonetheless embodies the spirit of what Hopper was seeking. Defining that particular mood, investigating his most characteristic sites, is what this search is all about.

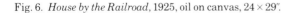

Fig. 6. *House by the Railroad,* 1925, oil on canvas, 24 × 29″.

NEW YORK AND ENVIRONS

Born in Nyack, New York, a small town on the Hudson River some forty miles north of New York City, Hopper was naturally drawn to the metropolis, with its museums, art schools, galleries, theaters, and other cultural institutions. After graduating from high school in Nyack in 1899, he traveled to New York daily, taking the train and a ferryboat across the Hudson, in order to study commercial illustration. Two years later, while attending the New York School of Art, Hopper began to study painting seriously. By the time he finished art school in 1906, he was already working part time as an illustrator for an agency in the city. After his three trips to Europe between 1906 and 1910, Hopper eventually settled in a modest studio at 53 East Fifty-ninth Street, although evidently he still spent much of his time at his family's home in Nyack. By the end of 1913, he had moved to a Greenwich Village studio at 3 Washington Square North, which would remain both his home and his place of work for the rest of his life. It was only natural, then, that New York City and its environs would figure importantly in his art.

Hopper made his first views of New York in his formative years, when he painted several canvases that depict scenes along the East River: *Blackwell's Island*

(now called Roosevelt Island) in 1911, *Queensborough Bridge* in 1913, and *East River* in about 1920–1923. By 1925, he had begun to produce watercolors of New York, such as *Manhattan Bridge* and *Skyline Near Washington Square*. During the next year, he continued to work in watercolor in New York, both in lower Manhattan and from the rooftop of his building: *Manhattan Bridge and Lily Apartments*, *Manhattan Bridge Entrance*, *Roofs of Washington Square*, and *Skylights*.

While fragmentary glimpses of New York buildings appeared in canvases like *New York Pavements* of about 1924, Hopper did not return to painting oils of specific New York views until *The City*, a 1927 painting of a corner of Washington Square, which he followed in 1928 with *Williamsburgh Bridge, Manhattan Bridge Loop*, and a second version of *Blackwell's Island*. Of course, most of the views Hopper painted in New York no longer exist, as new construction has replaced the small-scale older buildings he preferred to depict. Rarely do skyscrapers occur in his art, and when they are included, it is only in partial views.

My Roof, a watercolor Hopper did in 1928, continues his recording of views visible from the roof of his building. This composition features the skylight over the hall outside Edward and Jo's top-floor apartment. Four years later, in 1932, Hopper, working on his roof again, painted two canvases of his views: *City Roofs* (Pl. 1) and *November, Washington Square* (which he did not complete until 1959). Much of Hopper's roof view is preserved today, although some of the chimney pots have been removed and a massive new skyscraper fills the background. He probably became more interested in the view across Washington Square Park when he took over the studio facing the park in 1932, giving up his previous space in the back of the building to Jo. Although Judson Memorial Church remains intact, Washington Square below has been much altered by new construction.

During the 1930s and 1940s, Hopper ventured further afield and explored New York uptown. In 1935, after making many sketches along the East River, he painted *Macomb's Dam Bridge* in his studio. He also painted *Shakespeare at Dusk* in 1935, a view of monuments on the Mall in Central Park, with the skyline visible in the distance. In *Bridle Path* of 1939, he depicted another Central Park view, the uncharacteristic scene of three urban equestrians. *August in the City* of 1945 is set on the Upper West Side of Manhattan at Riverside Drive with Riverside Park visible in the distance. Closer to home, Hopper claimed that he was inspired to paint *Early Sunday Morning* in 1930 by shops on Seventh Avenue and *Nighthawks* in 1942 by a restaurant on Greenwich Avenue where two streets come together (Eleventh Street and Seventh Avenue). In the case of the latter, no such building has survived, while the former appears to resemble many places, none exactly right.

On occasion, in search of inspiration, Hopper took the Hudson River ferries to New Jersey, where *Sunday* (also known as *Hoboken Facade*) was set in 1926, or to Weehawken, where he made at least eight sketches for *East Wind Over Weehawken* (Pl. 2), which he painted in his studio in the winter of 1934. Today this street in Weehawken appears much as it did to Hopper, although the houses are painted in more subdued tones with much less polychrome. The lamp posts have been modernized, and some of the ornaments have changed.

Farther up the Hudson, Hopper was inspired by his hometown of Nyack, which offered a wide variety of architecture. As a boy he had sketched boats in the Hudson and painted a small watercolor of the view upriver to Hook Mountain. Around 1919, he painted an oil of the stairway in his family's home, revealing how skillfully he combined observation with his imagination. The architecture he portrayed resembles the house (now the Edward Hopper Landmark Preservation Foundation) as it looks today. If this is not immediately apparent, it is because Hopper took the liberty of inventing verdant rolling hills, mysteriously sus-

Fig. 7. *Summer Evening*, 1947, oil on canvas, 30 × 42″.

pended beneath an ambiguous field of blue, indicating either sea or sky, as the view out the front door—where one would actually see a flight of steps, the small front yard, and the street beyond. His choice of perspective, looking sharply down the stairs and out the door and then back up again, is also unusual. (Hopper would powerfully re-examine this theme in his 1951 canvas *Rooms by the Sea* [Pl. 24].) His *Summer Evening* (1947, Fig. 7) probably recalls a boyhood memory of his sister Marion, standing with a boyfriend on the porch of this house, for the basic layout of the porch structure, roof supports, windows, and door are identical.

A short walk up the street from Hopper's boyhood home in Nyack is a beautiful example of a Hudson River bracketed house, the home of Helen Hayes and her late husband, Charles MacArthur, who in 1939 commissioned Hopper to make a painting of it. Happy to have ceased working as an illustrator in the 1920s, Hopper did not enjoy working on commission. This is the only such assignment he ever accepted; that he reluctantly did so was due to the insistent nagging of his wife and his dealer, who considered this project important because of the celebrity status of the clients. Hopper made his working drawings at the house and then painted the canvas, *Pretty Penny*, in his New York studio. The result is a faithful rendering of the house he had complained he could not paint because the surrounding trees deprived it of light and air.

1. *City Roofs*, 1932. Oil on canvas, 29 × 36″.

2. *East Wind Over Weehawken,* 1934. Oil on canvas, 24½ × 50¼".

MAINE

Hopper first traveled to Maine to spend the summer of 1914 in Ogunquit, a coastal town not far north of Portsmouth, New Hampshire. He returned in 1915, and the following summer he visited Monhegan Island, a small island only a mile long and located twelve miles out to sea. Hopper had certainly heard his favorite teacher, Robert Henri, describe Monhegan enthusiastically after his first stay there in 1903, just at the time of Hopper's years of study under him: "a wonderful place to paint—so much in so small a place one could hardly believe it." And he was no doubt aware of journeys there made by his former classmates George Bellows, Rockwell Kent, and Julius Golz, among others. Like Henri, Hopper produced a number of small panel paintings of the unforgettable landscape of Monhegan, which features rugged, rockbound shores, dramatic towering headlands, thundering surf with sparkling crests and deep emerald eddies, flowering meadows, and dense forests.

At the summit of Monhegan, Hopper found the island lighthouse with its surrounding buildings worthy of an oil painting. He painted the site on location, working outdoors, just as he did when he produced his views of Blackhead, Gull Rock, and other island land-marks. Although the island today is nearly unchanged from the days when Hopper painted there, the wooden buildings surrounding the lighthouse have since been destroyed by fire, leaving only the old stone foundations as evidence of the other structures Hopper included in his composition. Today only the original lighthouse tower survives, a relatively short and squat stone structure surrounded by new wooden buildings.

Hopper was so enchanted by Monhegan, with its stunning, panoramic sea views, that he returned there for the next three summers, escaping the tedium of his work as an illustrator in New York. He explained: "Maine is so beautiful and the weather is so fine in the summer—that's why I come up here to rest and to paint a little, too." He continued to enjoy summers in Maine, although he sometimes preferred to return to Cape Ann in Massachusetts instead. Eventually, however, Jo talked him into summering on Cape Cod, which he came to appreciate because it stayed warmer there longer, offering Indian summers still good for painting outdoors after the crowds of tourists had departed.

After their courtship in Gloucester in 1923 and their honeymoon there in 1924, the Hoppers spent the next summer in Santa Fe, New Mexico, returning to Maine

in 1926. They traveled by train from New York, arriving first in Eastport (near the Canadian border), which did not interest them. Several days later, on July 6, from Rockland, Hopper wrote to his dealer, Frank Rehn: "We did not like Eastport at all. It has very little of the character of a New England coast town. We left after three days and went to Bangor by rail and then by boat to this town, a very fine old place with lots of good-looking houses but not much shipping."

Hopper happily reported making two "sketches" within two days, announcing what was to be an especially prolific period in his career, seven weeks spent in Rockland that summer, during which he went on to paint a number of watercolors: *Haunted House* (Fig. 1), a view of an abandoned nineteenth-century boardinghouse; *Talbot's House* (Pl. 4), a fine example of a Second Empire house with a mansard roof; *Civil War Campground,* the fields where Union recruits had bivouacked in 1861; views of the harbor, the railroad, the Lime Rock quarry, and a number of different trawlers in the shipyard.

Talbot's House, identified in Hopper's records as a "fine white mansard," is almost perfectly preserved today. Located within easy walking distance of the harbor, this stately house is now a home for the aged. Shrubbery has been added, and the view through the

Fig. 8. Hopper painting *Lighthouse Hill* at Two Lights, 1927.

porch to the adjoining land is no longer foliage but another house. Hopper's vantage point for this watercolor was the front step of a house located just across this quiet street, where he probably sat with his paper and paints. In his composition, he intentionally cropped the central tower, the top of the chimney, and the base of the house, creating the sense of an imposing image continuing beyond the boundary of the paper. The style of this house was one that had particularly appealed to Hopper over the previous three years, beginning with his watercolor *The Mansard Roof* (Pl. 11), painted in Gloucester in 1923.

By the next summer, 1927, the Hoppers had purchased their first automobile and could now roam about at will, without depending on train routes and schedules. They spent much of the summer on Cape Elizabeth in Maine, at Two Lights, just south of Portland. Hopper painted various views of the Coast Guard station, the surf, the lighthouse, the keeper's house, and the pictures titled *Lobster Shack* and *House of the Fog Horn* (Fig. 9). In nearby Portland, he also found a number of places to paint: the U.S. custom house (Pl. 9), the Libby house (Pl. 10), the lighthouse, the keeper's house, and the rocky shore. Uncharacteristically, he chose examples of outstanding architectural monuments as subjects for two of his watercolors, which usually focused on the vernacular.

Hopper was fascinated by this little Coast Guard set-

tlement at Two Lights, which, according to Jo, got its name because it used to have a second lighthouse. Jo later explained to the owner of one of his Two Lights pictures that the families of the Coast Guard men lived in the surrounding houses, but the men had to sleep in the station. Hopper was apparently intrigued by the isolation of their lives, which must have appealed to him personally. Probably at Jo's insistence, they managed to meet the residents of the houses he painted, prompting even the reticent Hopper to title his canvas *Captain Upton's House* (Pl. 6). Jo noted in the record book that in one of his watercolors, *Hill and Houses,* Captain Berry's house was located in the foreground and Captain Upton's was visible farther up the hill.

In Hopper's oil *Lighthouse Hill* (1927, Pl. 5), the lighthouse is shown with Captain Upton's house visible on the left, a view still preserved today. *Captain Upton's House* portrays a close-up view of the house from a different vantage point, with the tall tower of the lighthouse looming up just behind it. The outhouse and covered passageway leading to it have been torn down, and the lean-to shed has been replaced by a garage. Jo had remarked in a letter just how primitive life was at Two Lights, with "water from the village pump," meaning no indoor plumbing.

While the lighthouse and the keeper's house are nearly unchanged, the landscape surrounding them has undergone radical changes. Even in the last few

Fig. 9. *House of the Fog Horn II*, 1929, watercolor on paper, 14 × 20″.

years, new houses have been constructed on the land nearby, blocking some of the other views that Hopper painted here. No longer dominating a lonely isolated setting, this lighthouse now rests among a group of houses, looking decidedly suburban. The two small, red-roofed, white buildings Hopper painted in his watercolors *House of the Fog Horn I* and *House of the Fog Horn II* (Fig. 9) are still much the same, except for the now-truncated chimney, the instruments, which no longer project from the roof, the new chain-link fence, and a Danger sign. Moreover, the site is now bordered by a parking lot and a popular lobster restaurant.

Hopper painted several watercolors of the Portland lighthouse: one called *Portland Head-Light* (Pl. 7), showing the lighthouse and surrounding buildings seen from the summit of a large adjacent hill, with a vast sea stretching out beyond it; one called *Rocky Pedestal,* showing the base of the lighthouse perched on high rocks; and one called *Captain Strout's House* (Pl. 8), a frontal view of the keeper's home with the tower of the lighthouse partially visible behind it, blocked by the structure of the house and cropped by the top edge of the paper. These views are remarkably preserved today. The keeper's house has been painted in different colors, the building on the left has been replaced by a garage, the foghorn on the right has been removed, a garden has been added, and the fence has been replaced by one of a more complex design; but what Hopper recorded remains much as he saw it. The keeper's house still has a picturesque appeal linking man and the sea, which must have attracted Hopper.

In the city itself, where Hopper painted two watercolors, his subjects, the Custom House (Pl. 9) and the Libby house (Pl. 10), are well-preserved landmarks. The building that stood next to the nineteenth-century Custom House no longer exists, but even the curving utility pole still stands at the same corner location. Hopper must have liked the contrast of the angular shapes of the adjacent building with the flowing rhythms of the Custom House's graceful steps, arched windows, and cut-out fence. He abruptly cropped this large building to show only the front and the first story, in part to balance these shapes and patterns in his composition, and perhaps also to accommodate the close vantage point from which he worked on the corner across the street. Jo noted in the record book that Hopper painted this work in the rain, accounting for the pale palette, and probably indicating that he worked inside their parked car.

The Victorian mansion that Hopper depicted in *Libby House* is now a museum known as the Morse-Libby House. Until 1927, the very year Hopper painted it, the Libby family lived in this sumptuous home designed in Italian villa style in 1859 by the distinguished New Haven architect Henry Austin. In the years since, few changes have occurred: a tree is missing from the sidewalk at the side of the house, and a utility pole now replaces a large dead tree trunk that has been removed from the front sidewalk; a temporary awning has been added to the entranceway; shrubs have been planted; and a traffic sign stands on the corner. Hopper painted this scene in rather subdued tones, reflecting the strong sun bathing the structure with a harsh light. The overall composition of this house with its asymmetrical balancing of classical forms has a dramatic quality that must have attracted Hopper, who did not often select such elegant subjects. Hopper's fidelity to appearances is evident in his decision to include in his picture the very ordinary structure of the brick apartment building on the lot next door.

3. *Monhegan Lighthouse*, 1916–19. Oil on board, 9¹/₂ × 12³/₄″.

4. *Talbot's House,* 1926. Watercolor on paper, 14 × 20″.

5. *Lighthouse Hill,* 1927. Oil on canvas, 28¼ × 39½".

6. *Captain Upton's House,* 1927. Oil on canvas, 28½ × 36″.

7. *Portland Head-Light,* 1927. Watercolor on paper, 14 × 20″.

8. *Captain Strout's House*, 1927. Watercolor on paper, 14 × 20″.

9. *Custom House, Portland,* 1927. Watercolor on paper, 14 × 20″.

10. *Libby House*, 1927. Watercolor on paper, 14 × 20″.

GLOUCESTER

Hopper first summered in Gloucester, on Cape Ann, in 1912, where he painted with Leon Kroll, a friend from New York. That first summer he produced oils of the Italian quarter and Gloucester harbor, views that no longer exist, as the main waterfront area has changed considerably with the modernization of the fishing industry. Venturing farther afield, Hopper painted *Squam Light*, showing the lighthouse in Annisquam, just north of Gloucester. In all of these early canvases, he experimented with painting light and shadow to define structure.

Hopper was probably aware of other painters who had worked in Gloucester and of the town's history as a summer art colony. Beginning in the mid–nineteenth century, such artists as Fitz Hugh Lane, Sanford Gifford, William Trost Richards, Worthington Whittredge, Winslow Homer, William Morris Hunt, Frank Duveneck, John Henry Twachtman, and Childe Hassam had painted in Gloucester. But the Gloucester scenes Hopper certainly would have known were those by Maurice Prendergast, who had shown along with Hopper's teacher Robert Henri in the New York exhibition of "The Eight" in 1908. All of these artists appreciated Cape Ann for its intense sunlight, brightened by

the sea, and Hopper was no exception. He was also drawn to the local architecture, which offered wooden houses in a variety of distinctive styles ranging from shacks to ornate Second Empire mansions.

When Hopper returned to Gloucester during the summer of 1923 and encountered his former schoolmate Jo Nivison, he was prompted to take up painting in watercolor, if only to be a more compatible companion for their excursions. The blossoming romance and Hopper's proficiency in the medium both encouraged him to continue. He abandoned the opaque gouache that he had employed in his commercial work and explored the delicate transparency of watercolor, allowing the white of the paper to play a role in his composition. He developed a freer, more spontaneous way of handling paint and investigated luminosity with a new fervor.

That summer he spent much of his time in East Gloucester, exploring the Rocky Neck section and painting the lighthouse at Eastern Point. Jo noted in Hopper's record book that *Eastern Point Light* (Fig. 10) was his earliest watercolor painted outdoors. He chose for his location the same landmark painted earlier by Winslow Homer. Most of the buildings that Hopper

Fig. 10. *Eastern Point Light*, 1924, watercolor on paper, 14 × 20″.

painted surrounding the lighthouse are no longer extant, but the tower itself and its dramatic rocky setting are unchanged, still a popular spot for sunbathing, swimming, or painting.

Hopper painted *The Mansard Roof* (Pl. 11) in the Rocky Neck section of Gloucester, which even today is something of an artists' colony. He described Rocky Neck as "the residential district where the old sea captains had their houses" and later recalled that it had interested him "because of the variety of roofs and windows, the mansard roof, which has always interested me...." He also noted that he had "sat out in the street ...it was very windy" and offered: "It's one of my good watercolors of the early period." Actually, Hopper's view was from the back of the house, down toward the water, which must have increased the effect of the wind he so vividly recollected. Today the house is well preserved but missing the yellow awnings that he caught fluttering in the strong breeze. The foliage has grown up so that Hopper's view can be photographed only in winter or early spring.

Hopper returned to all of the places that he had painted in Gloucester in 1912, more than a decade earlier: near the lighthouse in Annisquam, he painted *Houses of Squam Light;* in the center of the town, he painted *Italian Quarter* and *House in Italian Quarter.* He then moved on to paint in other areas of Gloucester for the first time: *Shacks at Lanesville, Portuguese*

Quarter, and *Portuguese Church* (Our Lady of Good Voyage).

When Hopper painted *Gloucester Mansion,* the side view of a large, ornate Second Empire house set on a hill overlooking Gloucester harbor, and a year later painted this same imposing house in a frontal view as *Haskell's House* (Fig. 2), he was working in a location not far from where he painted his 1912 oil *Gloucester Harbor,* but his interests had led him to something much more personal than the picturesque harbor captured by so many artists before him. He now focused on this ornate hybrid style of American architecture which Jo called "the wedding cake house," a fitting subject for a work painted on their honeymoon.

Although painted in a completely different color scheme, the structure of this house today is just as Hopper depicted it. Yet the overall appearance is so changed that one does not initially recognize it. Unlike the house of *The Mansard Roof,* still set in a quiet corner of Rocky Neck, this once stately house is on one of busy Gloucester's main thoroughfares, overlooking the now industrialized harbor. The short shrubs that once lined the long steps leading up the hill to the house have been replaced by tall fir trees which totally block the view that Hopper painted.

Jo and Edward returned to Gloucester in autumn 1926, after their seven-week stay in Rockland, Maine, and remained there through October. Hopper worked in the center of town, concentrating on individual houses, with occasional ventures farther afield, to paint *House by Squam River* and *Trees, East Gloucester,* which he rendered in an unusually free and fluid style that Jo described as "wild and wooly."

More characteristic of this visit is *Anderson's House* (Pl. 13), which depicts a typical Gloucester three-story wooden house raked by sunlight. Today it is painted a different color and missing its shutters, but even the surrounding houses are intact, although the one in the distance no longer has a red roof. At the top of his composition, Hopper cleverly cropped the house's gable, pushing the viewer's eye back down to the repeated rectangular shapes below.

On Middle Street, across from the Davis house (Pl. 14), Hopper found a convenient churchyard in which to work without intruding on someone's front steps as he had in Rockland while painting *Talbot's House.* He later said that so many artists were working in front of the Davis house painting the church that he decided to sit in the churchyard and paint the house! The house is now white and the trees are gone, replaced by low shrubbery. Hopper compressed the pictorial space, so that the railing alongside the churchyard appears to be directly in front of the house instead of across the street. By cropping the house along the left side, he created a sense of continuity, the feeling that the scene goes on beyond the boundaries of his composition.

During September, working outdoors at the nearby corner of Church and Pine streets, Hopper painted *Gloucester Street* (Pl. 12), depicting three houses with gables in the foreground and a fourth building in the distance. This canvas resembles the watercolors in subject matter and composition, with cropped buildings on both sides. Today, except for color, this row of houses appears much the same as it did to Hopper. Only incidental changes have occurred: the picket fence across the street is now chain link; the houses have lost their shutters; arched windows have been replaced by cheaper rectangular ones; picket fences and railings have been added. The play of sunlight falling on the architecture still animates the scene with light and shadow, although the bright polychrome Hopper depicted has now been replaced by a uniform white, calling less attention to the houses' eccentric forms and individuality.

In 1928 the Hoppers spent their last summer in Gloucester, and Edward not only painted watercolors but also produced three canvases: *Freight Cars, Gloucester; Cape Ann Granite,* a view of a rocky pasture; and *Hodgkin's House,* located on the road to Annisquam. The watercolors Hopper painted at this time also include scenes of a pasture, railroad gates, a box factory, and a circus wagon, as well as the usual views of local streets and houses. The latter are well preserved today, looking very much as Hopper recorded them.

House on Middle Street (Pl. 15) records Hopper's return to the same road where he painted *Davis House* two years earlier. Although painted in different colors, this house looks nearly identical to Hopper's image except that he made it appear proportionately less wide and it is now missing its shutters and striped awnings. The grassy area to the left is now a paved driveway with steps leading down to it; on the right, the houses in the distance are painted brighter colors, and a tree has been added. It is interesting to note that even the utility pole on the right side remains in the identical position.

Prospect Street still appears as it did when Hopper painted it in 1928 (Pl. 16), with the towers of Our Lady of Good Voyage in the distance. The sun porch of the house in the foreground has been enclosed, and other houses on the street have new roofs and different colors, but the basic look remains the same. Street lamps and traffic signs have been added; the tops of the church's twin towers are now bright blue; and the cars are updated from the 1920s. Light and shadow still play upon the rhythmic shapes of gables, roofs, projecting doorways, and dormer windows to create the varied composition of visual shapes that appealed to Hopper.

The subject of *Adam's House* (Pl. 17), situated on a high hill overlooking the town below, also remains just about as it looked when Hopper painted his watercolor. Even the locations of the yellow fire hydrant and the utility pole are unchanged. Only the ornament that hung over the doorway is missing, replaced by an additional pair of shutters and a trellis at the entrance. The large tree in the yard on the left has disappeared, and the style of the picket fence has changed; but the view of Gloucester beyond is essentially the same. The contrast of the foreground with the distant panoramic view of the town below makes this a particularly interesting composition.

We might ask why Hopper, after so many fruitful experiences in Gloucester, was never again to spend any time painting there after the summer of 1928. A brief visit to friends in Ogunquit that summer probably prompted him to return to Maine for the summer of 1929, and the next year Jo finally persuaded him to try Cape Cod. Then, too, it is more than likely that Hopper had begun to be a bit bored with Gloucester, which, after all, he had thoroughly explored. New places meant fresh stimuli for him, and he often felt the necessity to go out and seek such inspiration.

11. *The Mansard Roof*, 1923. Watercolor on paper, 13¾ × 19″.

12. *Gloucester Street*, 1926. Oil on canvas, 28 × 36″.

13. *Anderson's House*, 1926. Watercolor on paper, 14 × 20″.

14. *Davis House,* 1926. Watercolor on paper, 14 × 20″.

15. *House on Middle Street*, 1928. Watercolor on paper, 14 × 20″.

16. *Prospect Street, Gloucester*, 1928. Watercolor on paper, 14 × 20″.

17. *Adam's House*, 1928. Watercolor on paper, 16 × 25″.

CAPE COD

In the summer of 1930, the Hoppers drove out to the East End of Cape Cod and rented in South Truro a modest cottage, which Jo described as "on the side of a hill in such a wonderful land of bare green sandy hills." They returned to this small, isolated house for the next three summers and came to call it "Bird Cage Cottage," because rain, wind, and animals entered it with equal freedom. Jo described their summer home as being "as primitive as the land it's in." The unusually bad weather during the summer of 1933 and a small, unexpected inheritance from Jo's family encouraged the Hoppers to build their own simple South Truro home with a studio space that enabled them to paint indoors. Situated on a cliff overlooking the bay, the new house, which Edward designed, was completed in the summer of 1934, at the time of their tenth wedding anniversary. It was not, however, until 1954 that they added electricity.

During his first years on Cape Cod, Hopper was inspired to depict his new surroundings, often recording them from the vantage point of his automobile. He walked and drove around finding many vistas that appealed to him. These included the tiny local railroad station (Fig. 4), the post office, buildings on the farm owned by their landlord, Burly Cobb, neighboring houses, farms, roads, the lighthouse in North Truro, and the bridge in nearby Wellfleet. He drove all the way to Provincetown, on the tip of the Cape, and there painted the Methodist Church tower and some of the local houses. He often painted along the railroad embankment and depicted the tracks crossing this remote countryside of Cape Cod's East End. Although Hopper never painted a view of the house he designed, Jo made various sketches and paintings of what she referred to as "Chez Hopper."

Some of the most imposing structures on Cape Cod have disappeared since Hopper depicted them, just as his views of the landscape have been changed by the unrelenting forces of nature. In 1930, he and Jo both painted views of the South Truro Church, which burned down in 1937. In North Truro in 1933, he painted an imposing, factorylike structure used as a fish warehouse until it was torn down (*Cold Storage Plant,* Fig. 5). Yet nature still held some interest for Hopper, and he occasionally depicted landscapes with cows grazing, sand dunes, or trees, although the latter were sometimes shown dead. It was not long, however, before he grew bored with the scenery that he had come to know so intimately.

Fig. 11. *Highland Light*, 1930, watercolor on paper, 16 × 25".

The North Truro lighthouse tower and keeper's house that Hopper depicted in a 1930 watercolor, *Highland Light* (Fig. 11), remain much as they were when he painted them, although some of the smaller outbuildings have been removed and fences have been added, blocking access and his original vantage point. The drama of this isolated spot overlooking the sea remains, as do the explosive Cape skies which silhouette the lighthouse tower.

The model for *Rich's House* (Pl. 18), in South Truro, looks much the same as when Hopper painted it in 1930. The new roof is a different color, and a large tree and some shrubs have grown up beside the house. Only the base of the windmill tower still stands, and the white picket fence is now of a slightly different design. In 1931 Hopper returned to this farm and painted the barn, another large white structure. As in almost all of Hopper's Cape Cod paintings, the forms are defined by the Cape's intense sunlight, which almost evokes the sense of being at sea.

Hopper painted *Dauphinée House* (Fig. 12) on canvas in 1932, having portrayed the subject in watercolor as *Captain Kelly's House* a year earlier. Jo, too, produced an oil of this house, which stood just by the railroad tracks, only a short walk from their home. Hopper painted it in watercolor once again in *Railroad Embankment* (1932). Eventually, the house was purchased by Hopper's friend and fellow artist Henry

Varnum Poor. Although grey shingles have been added to one side of this house, the shutters are painted a darker color, and shrubbery has been planted, the house still stands alone, isolated in a clearing, its simple geometric structure in sharp contrast to the gentle curves of the surrounding hills.

The Hoppers' nearest neighbors on the Cape were the Jenness family (Kelley, Harriet, and their daughter, Virginia), who came down every summer from Boston. They gave the Hoppers the use of their home for over two months during the spring of 1934, when Edward and Jo wanted to be present for the construction of their new house. Hopper, in exchange for this and the right-of-way over the Jennesses' land, promised to paint them a watercolor, a view of their home, which he had first depicted as *Kelley Jenness House* in 1932. Eventually, Hopper kept his promise, although this commitment weighed upon him, as he was reluctant to produce anything on demand. Today the simple structure of the Jenness home, set in the gently rolling hills, appears much the way it looked when Hopper painted his four versions of it (Pl. 19). Only the chicken coop or shed on the right side has been removed, and the new roof is a different color. The tall timothy grass, which grows abundantly in the sandy Cape soil, still turns the same golden-brown tones that Hopper painted.

Remarkably, the weather-beaten shacks in *Near the*

Fig. 12. *Dauphinée House*, 1932, oil on canvas, 34 × 50″.

Fig. 13. Edward and Jo Hopper on Cape Cod, c. 1930.

Back Shore (Pl. 20), a watercolor of 1936, have survived almost exactly as Hopper painted them nearly fifty years ago. Even the utility pole appears to lean at the same precarious angle. The sand dunes he depicted lead to the ocean beach in Truro, where Hopper did not often go, as he enjoyed swimming at the convenient bay beach just below his own house, and perhaps preferred to avoid other people, who were more likely to frequent the more beautiful ocean beach.

Hopper painted two watercolors of a house at the end of Station Road (today called Depot Road), not far from his home: *House with a Rain Barrel* (1936) and *Mouth of Pamet River—Fall Tide* (1937, Pl. 21). He wanted to depict the flood tide in the latter version, but he had to work fast, as the tide was quickly changing. He was also interested in other aspects of this bare, isolated setting, particularly the high sea grass in the surrounding meadows. Today the structure of the house remains relatively unchanged, but trees and shrubs have tamed the character of these once wild meadows, altering the somber mood and dramatic effect of the landscape that originally attracted Hopper.

And progress has not always been kind to Cape Cod. Development has reached even the more remote areas on the far end of the Cape. New houses now crowd the once spare landscapes Hopper knew, blocking the vistas. Hopper painted *Cottages of North Truro* (Pl. 22) in 1938, and everything he depicted survives; however, a new house has been inserted into the landscape. The railroad no longer goes to Cape Cod; the tracks he once painted in a canvas called *New York, New Haven, and Hartford* have been removed. The embankment and the track beds linger on, serving no purpose, however, but merely marking the landscape.

The quaint Provincetown boardinghouse on Bradford Street that Hopper captured in 1945 in *Rooms for Tourists* (Pl. 23) looks unchanged today, with the exception of the colors of the shutters and awnings and the position of the sign. Hopper depicted this house at night, contrasting the inviting, illuminated interior with the ominous darkened street outside. As with most of his later oils, Hopper made his preliminary drawings while sitting in his car and then produced the painting in his studio.

In 1951 Hopper produced *Rooms by the Sea* (Pl. 24), one of his most unusual paintings, inspired by the real view through the door of his Cape Cod studio. Looking out, one actually sees across the edge of the dunes to the vast expanse of the bay; but at Hopper's artificially chosen angle, only the sky and the water are visible—a magical vision of a doorway dropping off directly into the sea. Although the room visible in the distance is located in a spatial configuration identical to the Hoppers' bedroom, he moved the hinge of the outside door from the left to the right side. Here reality has been adjusted to serve the artist's fantasy, yielding to his imagination. In this work Hopper created a memorable drama evoking untold mystery.

18. *Rich's House*, 1930. Watercolor on paper, 16 × 25″.

19. *Jenness House Looking North*, 1934. Watercolor on paper, 20 × 28".

20. *Near the Back Shore*, 1936. Watercolor on paper, 14 × 20″.

21. *Mouth of Pamet River—Fall Tide*, 1937. Watercolor on paper, 20 × 28″.

22. *Cottages at North Truro*, 1938. Watercolor on paper, 19³/₄ × 27³/₄″.

23. *Rooms for Tourists*, 1945. Oil on canvas, 30 × 40″.

24. *Rooms by the Sea*, 1951. Oil on canvas, 29 × 40″.

CREDITS

Pl. 1. *City Roofs,* collection of Mr. and Mrs. George Strichman; photograph courtesy of Kennedy Galleries, Inc., New York.

Pl. 2. *East Wind Over Weehawken,* Pennsylvania Academy of Fine Arts, Philadelphia; Collections Fund Purchase.

Pl. 3. *Monhegan Lighthouse,* private collection; photograph courtesy of Kennedy Galleries, Inc., New York.

Pl. 4. *Talbot's House,* private collection.

Pl. 5. *Lighthouse Hill,* Dallas Museum of Art; gift of Mr. and Mrs. Maurice Purnell, 1958.9.

Pl. 6. *Captain Upton's House,* private collection.

Pl. 7. *Portland Head-Light,* Museum of Fine Arts, Boston; bequest of John T. Spaulding.

Pl. 8. *Captain Strout's House,* Wadsworth Atheneum, Hartford, Conn.; Ella Gallup Sumner and Mary Catlin Sumner Collection.

Pl. 9. *Custom House, Portland,* Wadsworth Atheneum, Hartford, Conn.

Pl. 10. *Libby House,* Fogg Art Museum, Harvard University, Cambridge, Mass.; purchase, Louise E. Bettens Fund.

Pl. 11. *The Mansard Roof,* Brooklyn Museum, New York; Museum Collection Fund.

Pl. 12. *Gloucester Street,* private collection; photograph by Kevin Clarke.

Pl. 13. *Anderson's House,* Museum of Fine Arts, Boston; bequest of John T. Spaulding.

Pl. 14. *Davis House,* collection of Harriet and Mortimer Spiller.

Pl. 15. *House on Middle Street,* Currier Gallery of Art, Manchester, N.H.

Pl. 16. *Prospect Street, Gloucester,* private collection.

Pl. 17. *Adam's House,* Wichita Art Museum, Kansas; Roland P. Murdock Collection.

Pl. 18. *Rich's House,* private collection.

Pl. 19. *Jenness House Looking North,* John and Mable Ringling Museum of Art, Sarasota, Fla.; photograph courtesy of Kennedy Galleries, Inc., New York.

Pl. 20. *Near the Back Shore,* collection of Janet S. Fleisher, Philadelphia, Pa.

Pl. 21. *Mouth of Pamet River—Fall Tide,* collection of Thelma Z. and Melvin Lenkin; photograph courtesy of Wunderlich & Co., Inc., New York.

Pl. 22. *Cottages at North Truro,* collection of Mr. and Mrs. Barney A. Ebsworth.

Pl. 23. *Rooms for Tourists,* Yale University Art Gallery, New Haven,

Conn.; bequest of Stephen Carlton Clark, B.A. 1903.

Pl. 24. *Rooms by the Sea,* Yale University Art Gallery, New Haven, Conn.; bequest of Stephen Carlton Clark, B.A. 1903.

Fig. 1. *Haunted House,* painting and photograph, William A. Farnsworth Library and Art Museum, Rockland, Maine.

Fig. 2. *Haskell's House,* private collection.

Fig. 3. *House on Dune Edge,* collection of Mr. and Mrs. George Strichman; photograph courtesy of Kennedy Galleries, Inc., New York.

Fig. 4. *Towards Boston,* private collection; photograph courtesy of Kennedy Galleries, Inc., New York.

Fig. 5. *Cold Storage Plant,* Fogg Art Museum, Harvard University, Cambridge, Mass.; purchase, Louise E. Bettens Fund.

Fig. 6. *House by the Railroad,* Museum of Modern Art, New York.

Fig. 7. *Summer Evening,* collection of Mr. and Mrs. Gilbert H. Kinney.

Fig. 9. *House of the Fog Horn II,* Museum of Fine Arts, Boston.

Fig. 10. *Eastern Point Light,* private collection.

Fig. 11. *Highland Light,* Fogg Art Museum, Harvard University, Cambridge, Mass.; purchase, Louise E. Bettens Fund.

Fig. 12. *Dauphinée House,* private collection.

Among the many people who have helped me to produce this book, the artist Ellen K. Levy deserves my deepest gratitude both for her continuing encouragement of my work as a photographer and for her invaluable insights on painting. My knowledge of Hopper owes a debt to the pioneering work of Lloyd Goodrich, who generously shared with me his recollections and expertise and the record books bequeathed to him by Hopper's widow. I have also benefited from discussions with many other friends and colleagues, particularly Raphael Soyer, Greta Berman, and David Bourdon.

On location, longtime Cape Cod residents Joan Lebold Cohen and Diana Worthington provided important assistance; in Gloucester, Nancy Miller helped me in my search, as did the local firemen. In Maine, Judy Tick generously aided my quest. I appreciate the generous help of photographer Kevin Clarke. Others who have contributed in various ways to this project include Cynthia Adler, Arthur Cohen, Lawrence A. Fleischman, Mona Hadler, Helen Hayes, Robert Indiana, April Kingsley, Ron Peck, Christine Podmaniczky, Aaron Radin, Robin Radin, Sue Reed, John Rewald, Anton Schiffenhaus, Larry Schiffenhaus, Philip Sunshine, and Lisa Zappia.

I wish to thank Bob Gottlieb at Knopf, who offered useful advice and supported this project from its inception. To Kathy Hourigan, my special thanks for her early recognition of my work and for helping me realize this book. I have been very fortunate in having Susan Ralston as my editor; her enthusiasm, advice, and sensitivity have contributed significantly.

A NOTE ABOUT THE AUTHOR

Gail Levin is an art historian and scholar who was, from 1976 to 1984, the Curator of the Edward Hopper Collection at the Whitney Museum of American Art in New York. She lectures and teaches at museums and schools around the United States. As a photographer, she has had a one-woman show in Kingston, N.Y., and has participated in several group shows. She is now working on a critical biography of Edward Hopper and on a catalogue of twentieth-century American paintings in the Thyssen-Bornemisza Collection. Among Gail Levin's earlier publications are *Synchronism and American Color Abstraction, 1910–1925; Abstract Expressionism: The Formative Years; Edward Hopper: The Complete Prints; Edward Hopper as Illustrator; Edward Hopper: The Art and the Artist;* and *Edward Hopper.*

A NOTE ON THE TYPE

The text of this book was set in a film version of Century Schoolbook, one of several variations of Century Roman. The original face was cut by Linn Boyd Benton (1844–1932) in 1895, in response to a request by Theodore Low DeVinne for an attractive, easy-to-read type face to fit the narrow columns of his *Century Magazine.*

Composed by Characters Typographic Services, Inc.,
New York, New York

Printed and bound by Comproject b.v. Holland, Baarn,
The Netherlands

Design by Dorothy Schmiderer